California Rental Property Management How To Start A Property Management Business

California Real Estate Commercial Property Management & Residential Property Management

by

Brian Mahoney

Get Massive Money for Real Estate Now!

1. Private Lending and Hard Money (Text Manual) (similar guides have sold for $1,500.00 alone)

2. Real Estate Investing Guide (Text Guide)

3. Goldmine Government Grants (Video Training Program)

4. Residential Government Grant Programs (Video Training Program)

5. Commercial Government Grant Programs (Video Training Program)

6. Creative Financing (Video Training Program)

7. Expert Credit Repair (Video Training Program)

8. Million Dollar Video Marketing (Video Training Program)

9. Customer List Building (Video Training Program)

10. Massive Web Site Traffic (Video Training Program)

11. SEO Marketing (Video Training Program)

12. Bonus 1000 Package!!!

Just Hit the Link Below Right Now!!!

Don't Wait....You'll Wait Your Life Away...

http://www.BrianSMahoney.com

Get Our Massive Money Complete Internet Marketing Video Training Program at:

(Zero Cost Internet Marketing complete 142 video series)

$1,997 Megasized Money Making Marketing Program

ONLY $67 !!!!

https://goo.gl/Qed1dY

Join Our VIP Mailing List and Get FREE Money Making Training Videos! Then Start Making Money within 24 hours!

Plus if you join our Mailing list you can get Revised and New Edition versions of your book free!

And Notifications of other FREE Offers!

Just Hit/Type in the Link Below

https://mahoneyproducts.wixsite.com/win1

ABOUT THE AUTHOR

Brian Mahoney is a best selling author of over 300 business start-up guides, real estate investing programs and Christian literature. He started his company MahoneyProducts in 1992.

He served in the US Army and worked over a decade for the US Postal Service. An active real estate investor, he has also served as a minister for the Churches of Christ in Virginia and Michigan.

He has degree's in Business Administration and Applied Science & Computer Programming.

His books and video training programs have helped thousands of people all over the world start there own successful business.

http://www.briansmahoney.com/

DEDICATION

This book is dedicated to my son's
Matthew and Christian.
A blessing from God and the joy of my life.

ACKNOWLEDGMENTS

I WOULD LIKE TO ACKNOWLEDGE ALL THE HARD WORK OF THE MEN AND WOMEN OF THE UNITED STATES MILITARY, WHO RISK THEIR LIVES ON A DAILY BASIS, TO MAKE THE WORLD A SAFER PLACE.

Disclaimer

This book was written as a guide to starting a business. As with any other high yielding action, starting a business has a certain degree of risk. This book is not meant to take the place of accounting, legal, financial or other professional advice. If advice is needed in any of these fields, you are advised to seek the services of a professional.

While the author has attempted to make the information in this book as accurate as possible, no guarantee is given as to the accuracy or currency of any individual item. Laws and procedures related to business are constantly changing.

Therefore, in no event shall Brian Mahoney, the author of this book be liable for any special, indirect, or consequential damages or any damages whatsoever in connection with the use of the information herein provided.

Table of Contents

Chapter 1 Property Management Business Overview

Property Management Business Overview

Property Management

A Property Manager manages real estate both commercial and residential. His or her responsibilities are vast. A property manager could oversee and monitor...

* Getting a license

* Finding a property

* Purchasing a property

* Marketing to bring tenants into the properties

* Collecting rent & security deposits from tenants

* Getting Rental Contracts made and signed

* Employees and contracts

* Screen prospective tenants

* Dealing with problem tenants

* Moving out tenants

* Handling tenant complaints

* Maintenance of properties and contractors

* Keeping the Properties clean

* Property security

* Financial Management and record keeping

Property Management Business Overview

National Apartment Association Education Institute (NAAEI)

https://www.naahq.org/about/naaei

This National Apartment Association also provides education courses and certifications for professionals in the apartment industry.

The National Apartment Association Education Institute (NAAEI) offers these courses. NAAEI is the education arm of NAA. It provides a large-based education, training and recruitment programs to develop apartment industry leaders.

https://www.naahq.org/education-careers/find-a-course

Courses Offered

* Certified Apartment Manager (CAM)

* Certified Apartment Portfolio Supervisor (CAPS)

* Certificate for Apartment Maintenance Technicians (CAMT)

* Independent Rental Owner Professional Designation Course (IROP)

* National Apartment Leasing Professional (NALP)

Property Management Business Overview

Start-up Cost: $3,000-$5,000

Potential Earnings: $25,000-$50,000

Typical Fees:

$25 per hour or monthly retainer $500-$2,500

Advertising:

Zero Cost Online Marketing, Internet Marketing, Business Cards, Online classified ads, Website

Qualifications:

Experience in Property Management or college degree or certification in the field. Management & communication skills, bookkeeping & building maintenance knowledge.

Equipment Needed:

Computer, spreadsheet & management software, printer, internet access, wi-fi, phone.

Home Business Potential: Yes

Staff Required: No

Hidden Costs: Insurance Bonding

Property Management Business Overview

Business Models

Percentage of rent

This is the most common model. The property management company usually keeps 10-15% of the rent amount, and shares the rest with the property owner.

Fixed fee

This is the most common revenue model used by companies when monitoring empty homes or empty land sites.

Guaranteed rent

This property management business model is also used mostly for small units in high demand locations. Here, the company signs a rental agreement with the owner and pays them a fixed rent.

Revenue share

This model applies to the service apartment space and other commercial establishments, such as retail or business centers that generate revenue. In this case, the property manager signs an agreement with the property owner, with the right to convert the property into a revenue generating business such as a business center, service apartment, etc.

Property Management Business Overview

Getting A License

United States

Most states, such as New York, Texas, and Colorado, require property management companies to be licensed real estate brokers if they are collecting rent, listing properties for rent or helping negotiate leases and doing inspections. A property manager may be a licensed real estate salesperson but generally they must be working under a licensed real estate broker.

Most states have a public license check system on-line for anyone holding a real estate salesperson or real estate broker's license. A few states, such as Idaho, Maine, and Vermont do not require property managers to have real estate licenses. Other states, such as Montana, Oregon, and South Carolina, allow property managers to work under a property management license rather than a broker's license. Washington State requires property managers to have a State Real Estate License if they do not own the property.

Owners who manage their own property are not required to have a real estate license in many states; however, they must at least have a business license to rent out their own home.

Property Management Business Overview

Getting A License

Owners who do not live near the rental property may be required, by local government, to hire the services of a property management company.

In California, third-party apartment property managers must be licensed with the California Department of Real Estate as a Real Estate Broker.

A broker's license is required for any person or company that, for compensation, leases or rents or offers to lease or rent, or places for rent, or solicits listing of places for rent, or solicits for prospective tenants, or negotiates the sale, purchase or exchanges of leases on real property, or on a business opportunity, or collects rents from real property, or improvements thereon, or from business opportunities.

Chapter 2

Finding Real Estate in California

Quick & Easy Access to Foreclosure Real Estate

When Investing in California first you have to determine what county you want to purchase in. To help you decide below is a list of all counties in California with their population and square miles. After the list of all the counties, you get a Goldmine Rolodex of web site address of Wholesale Government Tax Sale Properties and More!

California Counties	**Population**	**Square Miles**
Los Angeles County	10,170,292	4,060
San Diego County	3,299,521	4,204
Orange County	3,169,776	790
Riverside County	2,361,026	7,208
San Bernardino County	2,128,133	20,062
Santa Clara County	1,918,044	1,291

California Counties	Population	Square Miles
Alameda County	1,638,215	738
Sacramento County	1,501,335	966
Contra Costa County	1,126,745	720
Fresno County	974,861	5,963
Kern County	882,176	8,142
San Francisco	864,816	47
Ventura County	850,536	1,846
San Mateo County	765,135	449
San Joaquin County	726,106	1,399

California Counties	Population	Square Miles
Stanislaus County	538,388	1,495
Sonoma County	502,146	1,576
Tulare County	459,863	4,824
Santa Barbara County	444,769	2,738
Solano County	436,092	828
Monterey County	433,898	3,322
Placer County	375,391	1,503
San Luis Obispo County	281,401	3,304
Santa Cruz County	274,146	446

California Counties	Population	Square Miles
Merced County	268,455	1,929
Marin County	261,221	520
Butte County	225,411	1,640
Yolo County	213,016	1,012
El Dorado County	184,452	1,712
Imperial County	180,191	4,175
Shasta County	179,533	3,786
Madera County	154,998	2,138
Kings County	150,965	1,390

California Counties	Population	Square Miles
Napa County	142,456	754
Humboldt County	135,727	3,573
Nevada County	98,877	958
Sutter County	96,463	603
Mendocino County	87,649	3,509
Yuba County	74,492	630
Lake County	64,591	1,258
Tehama County .	63,308	2,951
San Benito County	58,792	1,389

California Counties	Population	Square Miles
Tuolumne County	53,709	2,236
Calaveras County	44,828	1,020
Siskiyou County	43,554	6,287
Amador County	37,001	606
Lassen County	31,345	4,558
Glenn County	28,017	1,315
Del Norte County	27,254	1,008
Colusa County	21,482	1,151
Plumas County	18,409	2,554

California Counties	Population	Square Miles
Inyo County	18,260	10,192
Mariposa County	17,531	1,451
Mono County	13,909	3,044
Trinity County	13,069	3,179
Modoc County	8,965	3,944
Sierra County	2,967	953
Alpine County	1,110	739

California

As of the writting of this book, all of these websites are up and running. From time to time some will change their address. If a site does not come up sometimes using the root of the address works. For example if www.mystate.gov/wholesaleproperty does not work. Just go with www.mystate.gov/

California Tax Sale/Foreclosure PROPERTIES

COUNTY

LOS ANGELES

https://ttc.lacounty.gov/Proptax/auction_faq.htm

ORANGE

http://ttc.ocgov.com/proptax/pta/

SAN DIEGO

https://www2.sdcounty.ca.gov/treastax/taxsale/taxsale.asp

Locate Statewide California Properties

MLS

http://www.mls.com/search/california.mvc

California Real Estate Foreclosures with links to different cities on the landing page.

http://www.realtor.com/realestateandhomes-search/California

REALTOR

Links to California real estate properties by county and city.

UNITED STATES REAL ESTATE INFO

http://www.statelocalgov.net/50states-tax-authorities.cfm

http://www.brbpub.com/free-public-records/

www.RealAuction.com

www.GrantStreet.com

Locate Nationwide Foreclosure Auction Properties

http://www.bid4assets.com/

Bid4assets is an amazing website for quickly finding investment property. The landing page has a map of the United States and you can just move your mouse pointer over the state you are interested in to see if they have any property in their database.

Here are just a few of assets you can target on this site!

* County Tax Sales

* Bank Owned Property

* US Marshal

* Real Estate

* Coins

* $1 No Reserve Homes

Locate Nationwide Foreclosure Auction Properties

Http://www.realauction.com

Real Auction is another great website for instant access to property information.

Once on the landing page click "client sites".

They have 4 categories of information.

*** Tax Liens Auctions**

*** Tax Deeds Applications**

*** Foreclosure and Tax Deed Auctions**

*** Tax Deed Management**

Then chose from the states and counties that appear, that they have auction information.

How To Find Wholesale Real Estate

Commercial Real Estate Properties

City Feet

is a nationwide database of Commercial Real Estate Property

http://www.cityfeet.com/#

The Commercial Real Estate Listing Service

is a nationwide database of Commercial Real Estate Property

https://www.cimls.com/

Land . Net

is a nationwide database of land, commercial real estate for sale and for lease.

http://www.land.net/

Loop . Net

is a nationwide database of Commercial Real Estate Property

http://www.loopnet.com/

CHAPTER 3

FINANCING REAL ESTATE

8 Realistic Ways to Finance Real Estate

FINANCING REAL ESTATE

Welcome to Expert financing. I am going to show you several realistic ways to finance real estate. You are going to learn how to finance real estate with.

* VA LOANS

* PARTNERS

* INVESTMENT CLUBS

* CREDIT CARDS

* CORPORATE CREDIT

* EQUITY

* SELLER FINANCE

* HARD MONEY LENDERS

* AND FINALLY I SHOW YOU THE MONEY$!!

USING A VA LOAN

According to the web sites www.benefits.va.gov and www.military.com the current VA Loan amount is a whopping $417,000! What a lot of veterans don't know is that you can use that money to purchase not only your home, but investment properties. That is how I started my investing career. Purchasing multiple homes using my VA Loan.

FINANCING REAL ESTATE

Even if you are not a veteran, you can still partner up with one, who still has some money left on his or her VA LOAN.

If you are a Veteran, you will need to obtain a copy of your DD 214 and VA Form 26-1880 Request for a Certificate of Eligibility.

PARTNERS

This is another way I purchased a home. At the time I worked for the United States Postal Service. I had already purchased plenty of homes, so many of the workers were aware I had successfully invested in real estate. At break time I went around and ask people to partner up with me. I had multiple people offer to go in as a partner. I choose one and that house we rehabbed and flipped just two months after purchasing it. To this day it was the biggest gross profit on one deal, I have had. True I had to split it with my partner, but I would rather have half of something than all of nothing.

Having the combined resources of two people can be a great benefit, but it is not without it's challenges. If you are going to use a partner, no matter how close you are...GET EVERY THING IN WRITING.

FINANCING REAL ESTATE

Having a partner can dramatically increase the chance of a Bank lending money as well as having someone to split the work on rehabbing, should you decide to save money and make repairs yourself. But all this must be spelled out BEFORE you enter into a Agreement/Contract and purchase a home.

It helps if the person is like minded and understands the risks and benefits of investing, and truly understands the return on investment of a particular deal.

REAL ESTATE INVESTMENT CLUBS

Real estate investment clubs are groups that meet locally and allow investors and other professionals to network and learn. They can provide extremely useful information for both the novice and expert real estate investor. A top real estate club can provide a great forum to network, learn about reputable contractors, brokers, realtors, lawyers, accountants and other professionals. On the other hand, there are many real estate clubs designed to sell you. They bring in "gurus" who sell either on stage or at the back of the room, and as a result, the clubs typically profit to the tune of %50 of the sale price of the product, bootcamp, or training that is pitched.

FINANCING REAL ESTATE

I have purchased a ton of real estate books and real estate courses. Carlton Sheets, Dave Del Dotto, The Mylands, Seminar courses and much much more. I am not against any club bringing in a speaker who has a course. However I think there should be transparency to the members of the club.

There is certainly value in the networking that may come at one of these groups. But attend working to attain your goals and not necessarily the club's goal to sell you something. Some times both are the same thing. As a rule I usually leave debit cards at home the first time I attend an event. If there is a seller there with a "This day only offer" then I won't feel pressured to purchase. Plus most sellers can be convinced to sell at the discount offer price at a later time when you have had a chance to come down off the "sense of urgency emotional pitch" .

CREDIT CARDS

When using a credit card in real estate you must really do your homework on the deal. Dan Kennedy a world famous marketer once said "always stack the numbers in your favor". That's how you use a credit card. Look at the return on investment as compared to the long term cost of using a credit card and it's interest. Also I would recommend buying low cost homes that you can purchase and own free and clear.

FINANCING REAL ESTATE

No Mortgage Payment!!! My last 2 homes I have purchased have been cash deals. One home cost $1,500 and the other about $7,000. The first was a government property from HUD and the 2nd From a Bank. These institutions are unemotional about real estate and simply view a property as a non performing asset. The 2nd home was 4 bedrooms, 1 1/2 bath and a basement located in a farming community and came with a 2 car garage/shed and .6 acre(that is the size of a NFL football field) of land.

Later in this book I will show you how to find plenty of houses with amazing below wholesale prices and a formula for almost always finding a great deal.

CORPORATE CREDIT

Many people set up corporations to buy and sell real estate as an additional protection against liabilities. Other's create a corporation to mask personal involvement in property transfers and public records. Regardless of the use of a corporation, you can buy real estate with corporate credit as an alternative to using your own cash or IRA. By capitalizing on the credit rating of your corporation, you can buy real estate and build your corporate holdings portfolio.

Just remember that you can set up your corporation in a state that favors you the most for your real estate deals. Do your research. Most people like Delaware and Nevada, but you will have to decide if your home state or any other state is best for you and your business.

CURRENT EQUITY

Using the equity in your home for real estate investing is another way you can finance properties. You might use the money for a down payment or it may only be enough to cover the cost of some rehab repairs.

If you stick to the low cost home formula, you may have enough to purchase the entire house. A house is an investment that should appreciate in value as well as give a great ROI (Return On Investment). Whether you decide to flip the property or rent it out for positive cashflow.

If you have equity and it's not doing anything, then you may decide to make it a "performing asset" and use it as part of your real estate finance program.

FINANCING REAL ESTATE

SELLER FINANCING

Seller finance is where the seller of a free and clear property becomes your bank along with being the seller.

Advantages:

You get to purchase the property on terms that may be more beneficial for you. Seller gets monthly payments and the benefit of treating the sale as an installment sale thus allowing them to defer any capital gains taxes that may be due.

Disadvantages:

You may be locked into a mortgage with a pre-payment penalty or may not be able to resell the property immediately. This strategy is typically not meant for flipping but can definitely be used for that purpose if structured correctly.

Seller Finance is a known way to finance a property. That is why I have presented it in this book. But it is my least favorite because you now have a lingering relationship with your property. Your ability to make decisions regarding the property is limited and for that reason, I would don't go this route. However, like all types of financing, you have to ask yourself, "is the deal worth it."

FINANCING REAL ESTATE

I also prefer to work alone, but when a great deal came along, I sought out a partner to make it happen. Risk is usually relative to potential profit.

HARD MONEY LENDERS

A hard money lender is usually a individual or company that lends money for investment of a secured by the investment property.

Advantages:

Less red tape to get the money. You are dealing with people who understand the real estate investment business.

Disadvantage:

This is not a long term loan. The lender wants a return on investment, usually within a few months, a a year, or a few years. The interest rate on the loan is much higher than usual conventional banks.

Using hard money has a higher risk because the return on investment is due quicker. Therefore it is good idea not to use a Hard Money Lender, until you have a great deal of experience and confidence in being able to produce a return on investment.

SHOWING YOU THE MONEY

www.businessfinance.com (4,000 sources of money!)

www.advanceamericaproperty.com

http://www.cashadvanceloan.com/

www.brookviewfinancial.com

www.commercialfundingcorp.com

www.dhlc.com
(hard money for the Texas area)

www.equity-funding.com

www.bankofamerica.com

www.carolinahardmoney.com
(for real estate investors in North and South Carolina)

www.fpfloans.com

Chapter 4
Blueprint for Tenants

BLUEPRINT FOR TENANTS

A reminder for all matters and topics in this book consult an attorney or other qualified professionals.

Getting Rental Contracts made and signed

A rental agreement is a short-term contract, usually month to month. It can be written or verbal.

A lease is a written agreement that specifies the length and cost of the rent each month for that period.

You should have an attorney that specializes in lease agreements, make up your contracts.

If you decide to do it yourself here are web site s

that have templates for every state in the United States.

Nationwide Rental Lease Agreements

https://rentalleaseagreements.com/residential/

Rocket Lawyer Free Lease Agreements

https://goo.gl/vQGTEz

BLUEPRINT FOR TENANTS

How to Screen Prospective Tenants

Credit Score

Check the credit score of any prospective tenants. The credit score can show and ability to pay and a willingness to take responsiblity to pay obligations.

Steady Employment

Use paystubs and bank statements as proof of steady employment and the ability to pay.

Income Ration

Income ratio should be about 3 times the amount of the rent.

Background Check

For your safety and the safety of any other tenants, do skip on doing a background check.

BLUEPRINT FOR TENANTS

How to Screen Prospective Tenants

Prior Evictions

Check for prior evictions. Make sure another property manager is not trying to pass their problem off on you.

Valid Credentials

Make sure that all identification and credentials match up. Some times people attempt rent property in other peoples names.

References

Check references thoroughly. Make sure that family and friends are not posing as prior landlords or work supervisors.

Reason for Moving

Ask the prospective tenant what was his reason for moving from his last residence. It may give you some insight into what kind of tenant you are going to have.

BLUEPRINT FOR TENANTS

Money – Money - Money

Collecting rent

There are several way to collect rent. Below are a few of the more common and popular ones.

Online or ACH

automated clearing house payments

This is by far, the most convenient for you. One such company is Agile Payments.

https://www.agilepayments.com/

Drop Off Box

Just have a secured drop off box at a office on the property grounds.

By Mail

Make sure that the tenant is aware that payment by mail still has to be received by the due date.

BLUEPRINT FOR TENANTS

Money – Money - Money

Security Deposits

A security deposit is a sum of money held in trust. An earnest payment, or else, in the course of a rental agreement to ensure the property owner against default by the tenant and for the cost of repair in relation to any damage explicitly specified in the lease and that did in fact occur.

Do not spend the security deposits. This money will come in handy should your property be damaged and the tenant skips out of town.

BLUEPRINT FOR TENANTS

How to Handle Tenant Complaints

Make sure that tenants must put ALL COMPLAINTS in writing. Letter or email. Make no verbal agreements! Respond to complaints as quickly as possible. Make sure that any contract that responds to any proplem only makes repairs authorized by you.

Common Complaints and How to Handle Them

Neighbor Complaints

Start with a phone call and get the accused side of the story. If that does not work, do a field inspection to verify any complaint. If the complaint is valid, send the accused a letter citing what ever lease violation they have committed, and the consequences if such behavior continues.

Pests

Most common pest complaint is roaches, mice and bed bugs. First make sure that you begin with no pests. Call contractor or maintenance. Have the contractor or maintance person determine who or what is the cause of the pests.

If it is the resident, let them know that it is a violation of their lease and they may have to pay for future pest removal.

Plumbling

The most common plumbing complaint is a toilet clog. Have a maintance person or a contract repair the clog. Sometimes tenant flush things like diapers and other inappropriate things down the toilet. Make sure that your lease agreement forbids such behavior.

Temperature Control

Have your maintenance person check the temperature. Many states have regulations on temperature, so you might want to invest in temperature lock out devices that don't allow the tenant to set the temperature.

How to Handle Tenant Complaints

Appliances

A refrigerator, stove or dish washer are the most common appliance complaint. Refrigerator repairs have priority, because food can spoil.

Hire a good appliance repair man. A repair can often save a fortune compared to a replacement.

Grounds

Getting roof leak, dumpster full, grass cut or snow removal is a common complaint. If you have these jobs contracted out, request a before and after photo of work done. Ice is particularly dangerous. You could get sued if someone injures themselves slipping on your property. Make sure you have reliable snow removal in place. Your maintenance team or a contractor should be able to handle most complaints about the grounds.

BLUEPRINT FOR TENANTS

How to Handle Tenant Complaints

Preventative Maintenance & Summary

Have maintenance outlined in your lease. This will assist you in preventive maintenance.

* Remember, everything must be in writing.

* The complaint must be in writing.

* You must respond in writing.

* When will the work be done.

* Who will be doing the work.

* Tenants will not be allowed to select a contractor.

* No repair work will be done without your authorization.

* No verbal agreements.

* Document multiple request for the same work to help reduces frivoulous calls and requests.

* State that request gives you permission to enter the property.

BLUEPRINT FOR TENANTS

Dealing With Problem Tenants

"If you are brave enough to say goodbye, life will reward you with a new hello."

Paulo Coelho

Tenant Problems

No matter how good a job you do screening you still may come across a problem tenant. Sometimes a tenant might lose a job or have a death in the family. Something that changes their ability to meet their lease requirements. Here are some tenant problems you need to be prepared for.

Not Paying Rent

You are running a for profit business not a charity, and the rent must be paid in order for you to sustain your business. So when rent is missed what should you do? Follow the process. Each state has a legal process to follow. In some states, you serve a 3 day notice to evict. Followed by a court date. Every state has their own process. Learn your state's process and follow it to the letter.

BLUEPRINT FOR TENANTS

Dealing With Problem Tenants

"It's not you, it's me..."

Structure your lease so that if you have a problem tenant you can sent a notice to vacate by a certain date. Some landlords have to serve a notice to cease the violation before they can send a notice to vacate. So begin by making sure your lease is structured properly in the first place.

Probable reasons to call it quits with a tenant.

* Abusing The Dwelling

* Disturbing the peace and quiet

* Breaking occupant rules

It is much easier to remove a tenant that has not paid, then a tenant that is breaking lease laws. So make sure your lease is very detailed as to what the rules are and what will happen if the rules are broken.

Chapter 5 Expert Tips For Managing A Property

THE PROPERTY

Keeping the Property Clean

You should make your property is always clean. Curbside appeal can attract new tenants and make the tenants you have, desire to stay.

Have maintanance personnel make a routine inspection of the property to make sure that is trash and debris are taken care of.

Larger properties may require a commercial property cleaning service.

Keep your property landscaped and the grass at the proper length. Again this adds to the curb appeal.

Part of keeping your property clean is to have an extermination company keep your property free of unwanted pests, like rodents and roaches.

Property Security

The property should be well lit. Light helps deter crime. However good lighting might not be enough. You may need to hire a security service to patrol the grounds or at least be on call, depending on the crime in the area.

Tenants may move out, if they don't feel safe. So make your tenants feel protected. Having security on property can deter crime and give the tenants a better feeling of comfort.

THE PROPERTY

Financial Management and Record Keeping

Software

Recently property management software prices have lowered and that has increased it's popularity. Software technology is allowing property managers to save time and run a more efficent business. Below are some of the top property management software programs currently on the market. All information, copy and pricing was taken from their website.

Property management software

123LandLord

http://www.123landlord.com/

123Landlord allows you to manage all of your tenants and properties, collect payments and track rent due.

Currently has 5 versions.

	Monthly fee	Tenants	Properties
Free	free	2	2
Professional	$13	12	12
Premier	$29	50	50
Deluxe	$49	75	75
Enterprise	$79	Unlimited	Unlimited

Financial Management and Record Keeping

Acturent

Forms

Preloaded legal forms save you time and money.

Website

Acturent allows you to build a custom website for your organization at no extra charge.

Tenant Services

Advertise your availabilities online, accept online payments, online applications, and much more...

Offers service and support by email.

They charge a base fee of $5 a month plus .30 cents per unit.

https://acturent.com/

THE PROPERTY

Financial Management and Record Keeping

AppFolio

"AppFolio Property Manager is designed for property managers who want to automate, modernize, and grow their business. Whether you manage multifamily, single-family, student housing, HOA, condo, or commercial properties- or maybe you manage a mixed portfolio - our all-in-one cloud-based solution has features built specifically for you so you can streamline your workday and focus on your bottom line."

Residental 1.25 per unit a month

Commercial 1.50 per unit a month

Student Housing 1.25 per unit a month

Community Associations .80 per unit a month

http://www.appfolio.com/

CHAPTER 6

How To Buy a Property

Strategies to Making Your Offer

Strategies To Making Offers

In microeconomics total cost (TC) describes the total economic cost of production and is made up of variable costs, which vary according to the quantity of a good produced and include inputs such as labor and raw materials, plus fixed costs.

In English... you factor in as many external costs, not just the cost of the investment property.

In order to be successful when buying investment property, you have to be good at determining the Total Cost of a property.

1. Get Investment Property Market Value

Wholesale Real Estate is real estate that is real estate priced under it's retail value. But how do you know that the retail value of real estate property? The standard formula for finding the value of real estate is to have a real estate agent find comparable (comps) properties that have sold recently. Usually about 4 properties with in a mile of the purchase property, that have sold within the past year. Formulas vary from bank to bank and real estate agent to real estate agent.

Today you can get a rough estimate by doing the research yourself. Remember that a bank will probably use their own formula, but at least you can try to get a ball park figure of a properties value by using the web sites below.

Strategies To Making Offers

Appraisal Web Sites

https://www.zillow.com/how-much-is-my-home-worth/

http://www.eppraisal.com/

2. Selecting a Real Estate Agent

So now that you have found a property, researched it's value, it's time to make an offer. As I mentioned in a earlier chapter of this book, some times you have to use a government approved agent to make an offer. Like any profession, there are good agents and not so good agents.

When I lived in Virginia, once a year the local paper published a list of all the top real estate agents for almost every real estate agent franchise/business. If your local paper does not do that then here is a formula I use for selecting a real estate agent.

Strategies To Making Offers

No part timers. Part time effort usually gets you part time results. I want an agent whose livelihood depends on their success.

Size Does Matter

The size that matters. The size or amount of properties sold. Not necessarily the gross amount of property value sold. Suppose you had a real estate agent who sold 1 million dollars worth of real estate and another who sold $500,000 worth of real estate. Which one do you choose? It depends. I want the agent who has sold the most individual properties, and not necessary the one who has the highest gross. An agent can sell only 1 house for a million dollars. The agent who sold $500,000 worth of real estate may have sold 10 $50,000 homes.

Usually a agent who makes a lot of sales has a good marketing formula in place and a good team of agents working with or for her/him. Don't be afraid to ask "who's your best agent? Why?". Often a real estate company will try to toss their worst agent a bone. Don't be that bone. Remember they work for you. Their commission comes the the property you are investing in.

Some courses teach you to negotiate the commission. I believe a proficient agent is worth the commission they desire. It's your job to select a good one.

3. "100-3" Formula

Here is a quick and easy formula for getting a great deal on a real estate investment property, using a real estate agent that you have build up some rapport with.

Have the agent find 100 properties for sale that have been on the market for at least 90 days. Have the agent fax an offer of 25% below market value to all of the properties. Because the properties has been on the market for at least 90 days, you are dealing with a more motivated seller. It is likely that 10 out of the 100 will accept your offer.

Now filter through the 10 and select the best 3 properties. Use these filters to help you select the best 3.

Strategies To Making Offers

1. What are the property taxes?
2. Are the any Homeowner Association dues?
3. What will be the appreciation value?
4. What will be your utility expenses.
5. How much will it cost, to be live in ready.
6. Is it the lowest valued house in the neighborhood?
7. Crime Rate

Property Taxes

I once owned two homes free and clear. The homes were in the same state. Both were similar in size, but one had a $3,000 a year property tax and the other one was $300 a year in property taxes. You can guess which one I moved first. Property taxes are often overlooked, but can be a big factor in the (TC) total cost. Due your research before you make an offer.

HOA

Usually when a house seems like the perfect deal, but has been sitting on the market for a long time, look to see what the HOA dues are. Personally I stay away from any property that has HOA dues, because they can escalate and you have no control over them.

Appreciation

Look at the history of real estate appreciation. It can vary greatly form city to city, and neighborhood to neighborhood. If you are going for a quick flip then this is not that important.

Utility Expenses

The importance of the expense depends on what you are going to do with the property.

Strategies To Making Offers

Rehab Expenses

If you are not an expert, have a professional inspect the house so you can factor in, a accurate estimate of rehab expenses. Be aware of any possible code violations as well.

Cost relative to the Neighborhood

Usually it's easiest to sell the cheapest house in the most expensive neighborhood. However if you just plan on renting the house then this is not as big a factor.

Crime Rate

The crime rate can have a big impact on resale value. Use web sites like https://www.crimereports.com/ to help understand it's impact on your property.

Strategies To Making Offers

4. "Take what the defense gives you"

Take what the defense gives you is a sports metaphor for viewing the landscape of a situation and adapting to what you see.

Take a similar approach to making offers in real estate. If you tell a "For Sale By Owner" everything that is wrong with the house he or she spend a lifetime building... you may insult the owner and lose the deal.

However, you send a list of needed repairs to a HUD representative, he may reduce the price of the property, no questions asked.

Adjust your offer making strategy to the person or organization you are dealing with. The farther removed a person is from the property, the less emotional they are about making deals.

Know your profit numbers and stick to them. Especially if you are bidding on a property. Be aware of Auction fever. It will bring out the competative nature in you and can lead to you over bidding on a property.

Know your numbers and be disciplined. The reason you pick out 3 properties in the 100-3 formula is so that you have 2 other properties to go to, if your first choice does not work out.

CHAPTER 7

How to Sell Your Property Fast!

12 Steps to Selling Any Property Fast!

How to Sell Your Property Fast!

12 Steps to Selling Any Property Fast!

1. Clean and Paint the Property

Make sure the Property is clean and uncluttered. This makes it easier for buyer to envision themselves living there. Make the bathrooms and kitchen a priority.

2. Scent the Property

You might use a light incense or place some vanilla extract and place it on a old school lightbulb to give it a fresh baked cookie smell.

3. Write a property description

Writing a great property description is key to getting buyers interested in your home. One short cut to learning how to write a good property description is to view property listings of sold properties.

4. Take Good pictures

If you don't have a good camera, buy one. A picture is worth a 1,000 words.

12 Steps to Selling Any Property Fast!

5. Send a email to your buyers list

If you do not have a buyer's list, here is a link to a complete set of training videos on how to build a valuable customer list.

https://goo.gl/UFSIY6

6. Post ads on craigslist

Keep reposting your ads on a daily basis so that you stay at the top of the search results.

7. **Post ads to http://www.backpage.com/**

This is a Worldwide Classified Ad Web Site.

12 Steps to Selling Any Property Fast!

8. **Place a Ad on http://realeflow.com/**

This is the number one source for real estate investing leads.

9. https://www.zillow.com/rental-manager/

This is a free rental web site.

10. Create a video virtual tour

Create a video virtual tour and upload the video to YouTube. This is a powerful tool. YouTube is 2nd only to Google as the largest Search Engine in the world. However just posting a video won't get it seen. It has to be Search Engine Optimized(SEO). Below is a link to training videos that will show you step by step how to create great videos and get massive traffic viewing them!

https://goo.gl/UFSIY6

12 Steps to Selling Any Property Fast!

11. Post an ad on facebook target a city

You can place an ad on Facebook and target the city that your property is in.

12. Place a Standard For Sale sign in the yard

If posible have flyers available as well.

13. Place addition white signs in the yard

Give more information and get more attention by placing more personal signs in the yard.

14. List property in the MLS

If you are not a real estate agent get one to do it for you.

12 Steps to Selling Any Property Fast!

15. Place directional signs

Help people find your Property. Make sure you are not violating any county codes when placing signs.

16. Continue marketing until closing

Don't slack off. If necessary you might want to hire VA's Virtual Assistants to keep all ads running.

17. Eliminating Negative Cash Flow

https://www.airbnb.com/

Airbnb is a web site that markets your Property or rooms in your Property for rent. It's easier to sell your Property when it is clean, empty and buyers can envision themselves living in it.

However, if you are suffering from negative cash flow you might want to look into just renting out 1 room in the Property.

12 Steps to Selling Any Property Fast!

18. ZERO COST MARKETING

Below are a few steps to market anything using ZERO COST INTERNET MARKETING STRATEGIES.

While there are many ways to market. In this section we are only going focus on ZERO COST MARKETING. When you are more established you can always go for the more expensive ways of marketing after your business is producing income.

FREE WEB HOSTING

Get a free web site. You can get a free web site at weebly.com or wix.com. Or just type "free web hosting" in a google, bing or yahoo search engine.

Free web hosting is something you can use for a variety or reasons. However many free web hosting sites add an extension to the name of your web address, and that lets everyone know you are using their services. For this reason you eventually want to scale up once you start making income.

LOW COST PAID WEB HOSTING

Free is nice, but you when you need to expand your business it is best to go with a paid web hosting service. There are several that give you good value for under $10.00 a month.

19. Low Cost Paid Web Hosting

1. Yahoo small business
2. Intuit.com
3. ipage.com
4. Hostgator.com
5. Godaddy.com
6. Webhosting pad

Yahoo small business allows for unlimited web pages and is probably the best overall value, but they require a years payment up front. Intuit allows for monthly payments.

For free ecommerce on your web site, open up a Paypal account and get the HTML code for payment buttons for free. Then put those buttons on your web site.

20. More Zero Cost Marketing

Step 1 zero cost internet marketing

Now that your web site is up and running you should register it with at least the top 3 search engines.

1. Google 2. Bing 3. Yahoo.

Step 2 zero cost internet marketing

Write and submit a press release. Google "free press release sites" for press release sites that will allow you to summit press releases for free. If you do not know how to write a press release go to www.fiverr.com and sub-contract the work out for only $5.00 !!!

Step 3 zero cost internet marketing

Write and submit articles to article marketing web sites like ezinearticles.com.

Step 4 zero cost internet marketing

Create and submit videos to video sharing sites like dailymotion.com or youtube.com. Make sure to include a hyperlink to your website in the description of your videos.

Step 5 zero cost internet marketing

Submit your web site to dmoz.org. This is a huge open directory that many smaller search engines go to get web sites for their database.

University
Police

CHAPTER 8

REAL ESTATE TERMS

REAL ESTATE TERMS

Acceleration Clause - A contract provision that allows a lender to require a borrower to repay all or part of an outstanding loan if certain requirements are not met. An acceleration clause outlines the reasons that the lender can demand loan repayment. Also known as "acceleration covenant".

Accrued Depreciation - Depreciation is the loss in value to any structure due to a variety of factors, such as wear and tear, age, and poor location. The term accrued depreciation means the total depreciation of a building from all causes.

Accrued Interest - In finance, accrued interest is the interest on a bond or loan that has accumulated since the principal investment, or since the previous coupon payment if there has been one already. For a financial instrument such as a bond, interest is calculated and paid in set intervals (for instance annually or semi-annually).

Active Income - Active income is income for which services have been performed. This includes wages, tips, salaries, commissions and income from businesses in which there is material participation.

Add-on Interest - A method of calculating interest whereby the interest payable is determined at the beginning of a loan and added onto the principal. The sum of the interest and principal is the amount repayable upon maturity.

Adjustable Rate Mortgage (ARM) - A variable-rate mortgage, adjustable-rate mortgage (ARM), or tracker mortgage is a mortgage loan with the interest rate on the note periodically adjusted based on an index which reflects the cost to the lender of borrowing on the credit markets.

Cash flow after taxes (CFAT) - Cash flow after taxes (CFAT) is a measure of financial performance that looks at the company's ability to generate cash flow through its operations. It is calculated by adding back non-cash accounts such as amortization, depreciation, restructuring costs and impairments to net income.

Agent - One who is legally authorized to act on behalf of another person.

Agreement for sale - An agreement of sale constitutes the terms and conditions of sale of a property by the seller to the buyer. ... Sale deed is the document prepared at the time of full payment made by the buyer and when the actual transfer of the property takes place.

REAL ESTATE TERMS

Alienation clause - A clause in a mortgage contract that requires full payment of the balance of a mortgage at the lender's discretion if the property is sold or the title to the property changes to another person. Nearly all mortgages have an alienation clause.

All-inclusive deed of trust (AITD) - An All Inclusive Trust Deed (AITD) is a new deed of trust that includes the balance due on the existing note plus new funds advanced; also known as a wrap-around mortgage.

American Land Title Association (ALTA) -The American Land Title Association (ALTA) is a trade association representing the title insurance industry. Founded in 1907, ALTA also focuses on a property's abstract of title, which ties the history of the title to a particular piece of real estate.

Amortization - Amortization is an accounting term that refers to the process of allocating the cost of an intangible asset over a period of time. It also refers to the repayment of loan principal over time.

Amortized loan - An amortized loan is a loan with scheduled periodic payments that consist of both principal and interest. An amortized loan payment pays the relevant interest expense for the period before any principal is paid and reduced.

REAL ESTATE TERMS

Appraisal - an expert estimate of the value of something.

Appraised value - An appraised value is an evaluation of a property's value based on a given point in time that is performed by a professional appraiser during the mortgage origination process. The appraiser is usually chosen by the lender, but the appraisal is paid for by the borrower.

Appraiser - A practitioner who has the knowledge and expertise necessary to estimate the value of an asset, or the likelihood of an event occurring, and the cost of such an occurrence.

Arbitration - the use of an arbitrator to settle a dispute.

Arbitration clause - An arbitration clause is a clause in a contract that requires the parties to resolve their disputes through an arbitration process

Asking price - the price at which something is offered for sale.

Assessment - the evaluation or estimation of the nature, quality, or ability of someone or something.

Assignee - a person to whom a right or liability is legally transferred.

Assignment - An assignment (Latin cessio) is a term used with similar meanings in the law of contracts and in the law of real estate. In both instances, it encompasses the transfer of rights held by one party—the assignor—to another party—the assignee.

Assumption Clause - A provision in a mortgage contract that allows the seller of a home to pass responsibility to the buyer of the home for the existing mortgage. In other words, the new homeowner assumes the existing mortgage. There are typically many conditions and a fee required in an assumption clause.

Assumption of mortgage - Mortgage assumption is the conveyance of the terms and balance of an existing mortgage to the purchaser of a financed property, commonly requiring that the assuming party is qualified under lender or guarantor guidelines.

At-risk rule - Tax laws limiting the amount of losses an investor (usually a limited partner) can claim. Only the amount actually at risk can be deducted.

Authorization to sell - Authorization to sell is a listing contract whereby a representative is employed by a seller to secure a buyer for the property. An authorization to sell does not give the agent the authority to enter into a binding contract of sale.

Backup offer - A backup offer is when a home seller has accepted an offer from a buyer, but is still accepting offers from other buyers. Sellers state that they are accepting backup offers if they think the current offer may fall through

Balloon mortgage - a mortgage in which a large portion of the borrowed principal is repaid in a single payment at the end of the loan period.

Balloon payment - a repayment of the outstanding principal sum made at the end of a loan period, interest only having been paid hitherto.

Binder insurance - binder. A legal agreement issued by either an agent or an insurer to provide temporary evidence of insurance until a policy can be issued. Binders should contain definite time limits, should be in writing, and should clearly designate the insurer with which the risk is bound

Capital gain - a profit from the sale of property or of an investment.

Capitalization - the provision of capital for a company, or the conversion of income or assets into capita

Cash basis taxpayer - A taxpayer who reports income and deductions in the year that they are actually paid or received. Cash basis taxpayers cannot report receivables as income, nor deduct promissory notes as payments.

Cash flow - the total amount of money being transferred into and out of a business, especially as affecting liquidity.

Certificate of title - A certificate of title is a state or municipal-issued document that identifies the owner or owners of personal or real property. A certificate of title provides documentary evidence of the right of ownership.

Chattel - an item of property other than real estate.

Closing costs - Closing costs are fees paid at the closing of a real estate transaction. This point in time called the closing is when the title to the property is conveyed (transferred) to the buyer. Closing costs are incurred by either the buyer or the seller.

Cloud on title - Any document, claim, unreleased lien or encumbrance that might invalidate or impair the title to real property or make the title doubtful. Clouds on title are usually discovered during a title search. Clouds on title are resolved through initiating a quitclaim deed or a commencement of action to quiet title.

Co-insurance - a type of insurance in which the insured pays a share of the payment made against a claim.

Collateral - something pledged as security for repayment of a loan, to be forfeited in the event of a default.

Commission - A fee charged by a broker or agent for his/her service in facilitating a transaction, such as the buying or selling of securities or real estate. In the case of securities trading, brokers can be split into two broad categories depending on the commissions they charge.

Contract of sale - A real estate contract is a contract between parties for the purchase and sale, exchange, or other conveyance of real estate.

Cost approach - Cost approach. ... The fundamental premise of the cost approach is that a potential user of real estate won't, or shouldn't, pay more for a property than it would cost to build an equivalent. The cost of construction minus depreciation, plus land, therefore is a limit, or at least a metric, of market value.

Debt coverage ratio - In corporate finance, DSCR refers to the amount of cash flow available to meet annual interest and principal payments on debt, including sinking fund payments. In personal finance, DSCR refers to a ratio used by bank loan officers in determining debt servicing ability.

Declining balance method - A declining balance method is a common depreciation-calculation system that involves applying the depreciation rate against the non-depreciated balance.

Deed - A deed (anciently "an evidence") is any legal instrument in writing which passes, affirms or confirms an interest, right, or property and that is signed, attested, delivered, and in some jurisdictions, sealed. It is commonly associated with transferring (conveyancing) title to property.

Deed of trust - In real estate in the United States, a deed of trust or trust deed is a deed wherein legal title in real property is transferred to a trustee, which holds it as security for a loan (debt) between a borrower and lender. The equitable title remains with the borrower.

Depreciation - Depreciation is an accounting method of allocating the cost of a tangible asset over its useful life. Businesses depreciate long-term assets for both tax and accounting purposes.

Double escrow - Double escrow. ... Double escrow is a set of real estate transactions involving two contracts of sale for the same property, to two different back-to-back buyers, at the same or two different prices, arranged to close on the same day.

Due diligence - Due diligence means taking caution, performing calculations, reviewing documents, procuring insurance, walking the property, etc. — essentially doing your homework for the property BEFORE you actually make the purchase

Earnest money - Earnest money is a deposit made to a seller showing the buyer's good faith in a transaction. Often used in real estate transactions, earnest money allows the buyer additional time when seeking financing. Earnest money is typically held jointly by the seller and buyer in a trust or escrow account.

Eminent domain - Eminent Domain. The power of the government to take private property and convert it into public use. The Fifth Amendment provides that the government may only exercise this power if they provide just compensation to the property owners.

Encroachment - A situation in real estate where a property owner violates the property rights of his neighbor by building something on the neighbor's land or by allowing something to hang over onto the neighbor's property.

Equity participation - Equity participation is the ownership of shares in a company or property. ... The greater the equity participation rate, the higher the percentage of shares owned by stakeholders. Allowing stakeholders to own shares ties the stakeholders' success with that of the company or real estate investment.

Escrow - Escrow generally refers to money held by a third-party on behalf of transacting parties. ... It is best known in the United States in the context of real estate (specifically in mortgages where the mortgage company establishes an escrow account to pay property tax and insurance during the term of the mortgage).

Escrow instructions - n. the written instructions by buyer and seller of real estate given to a title company, escrow company or individual escrow in "closing" a real estate transaction. These instructions are generally prepared by the escrow holder and then approved by the parties and their agents. (See: closing, escrow)

Estoppel - Estoppel Certificate. An estoppel certificate is a document used in mortgage negotiations to establish facts and financial obligations, such as outstanding amounts due that can affect the settlement of a loan. It is required by a lender of a third party in a real estate transaction

Exclusive right to sell listing - An Exclusive Right to Sell/Lease means that the listing brokerage has an exclusive listing agreement with the Seller. (Sorry about using a word in the term to define the term!) It means that a commission would be owed to the Listing Brokerage when the property is sold to a buyer, regardless of who brings the buyer.

Fair market value - The fair market value is the price at which the property would change hands between a willing buyer and a willing seller, neither being under any compulsion to buy or to sell and both having reasonable knowledge of relevant facts.

Fee simple - In English law, a fee simple or fee simple absolute is an estate in land, a form of freehold ownership. It is a way that real estate may be owned in common law countries, and is the highest possible ownership interest that can be held in real property.

First right of refusal - A right of first refusal is a contractual right granted by an owner of property. The owner gives the holder of the right an opportunity to enter into a business transaction with the owner according to specified terms, before the owner may enter into that transaction with a third party.

Foreclosure - Foreclosure is a legal process in which a lender attempts to recover the balance of a loan from a borrower, who has stopped making payments to the lender, by forcing the sale of the asset used as the collateral for the loan.

Gift deed - Quitclaim Deed Vs. Gift Deed. Property deeds define and protect ownership in a home. In real estate, deeds are legal documents that transfer ownership of a property from one party to another. ... Each type of deed is used for a specific situation.

Grantee - In real estate, the grantee is the recipient of a property - the person who will be taking title, as named in the the legal document used to transfer the real estate. The person who is relinquishing the property is called the grantor.

Grantor - First, it's important to review the legal definition of "grantor" and "grantee." In a real estate transaction, the grantor is the party that conveys the property in question. The grantor may be an individual, business entity or partnership. The grantee is the party that receives the property

Gross income - A real estate investment term, Gross Operating Income refers to the result of subtracting the credit and vacancy losses from a property's gross potential income. Also Known As: Effective Gross Income (EGI)

Gross rent multiplier - Gross Rent Multiplier is the ratio of the price of a real estate investment to its annual rental income before accounting for expenses such as property taxes, insurance, utilities, etc.

Highest and best use - The Appraisal Institute defines highest and best use as follows: The reasonably probable and legal use of vacant land or an improved property that is physically possible, appropriately supported, financially feasible, and that results in the highest value.

Income approach to value - The income approach is a real estate appraisal method that allows investors to estimate the value of a property by taking the net operating income of the rent collected and dividing it by the capitalization rate.

Installment sale - A method of sale that allows for partial deferral of any capital gain to future taxation years. Installment sales require the buyer to make regular payments, or installments, on an annual basis, plus interest if installment payments are to be made in subsequent taxation years.

Insurable title - Marketable Title vs. Insurable Title. ... When a title is marketable it means that the chain of ownership (title) to a particular piece of property is clear and free from defects. And as such, it can be marketed for sale without additional effort by the seller or potential buyer.

Interest - Estates and ownership interests defined. The law recognizes different sorts of interests, called estates, in real property. The type of estate is generally determined by the language of the deed, lease, bill of sale, will, land grant, etc., through which the estate was acquired.

Internal rate of return (IRR) - Internal rate of return (IRR) is a metric used in capital budgeting measuring the profitability of potential investments. Internal rate of return is a discount rate that makes the net present value (NPV) of all cash flows from a particular project equal to zero. ... r = discount rate, and. t = number of time periods

Involuntary lien - involuntary lien. A lien on real estate that results without the property owners' voluntary cooperation in the placement of the lien. Examples include tax liens and judgment liens. Contrast with a mortgage,which is voluntary.

Joint and several note - Joint and several note is a promissory note which is the note of all and of each of the makers as to its legal obligation between the parties to it.

Joint tenancy - A type of property right where two or more people own or rent a property together, each with equal rights and obligations, until one owner dies. Upon an owner's death, that owner's interest in the property passes to the survivors without the property having to go through probate.

Judgment proof - People are judgment-proof if they lack the resources or insurance to pay a court judgment against them. For example, suppose that a thief steals your car, sells it, and then burns all of his worldly possessions. Even if you sued him and won, you could not recover anything because the thief is judgment-proof.

Lease option - A lease option (more formally Lease With the Option to Purchase) is a type of contract used in both residential and commercial real estate. In a lease-option, a property owner and tenant agree that, at the end of a specified rental period for a given property, the renter has the option of purchasing the property.

Letter of credit - 1. INTRODUCTION. Letters of credit are often used in real estate transactions to secure obligations. ... For example, a tenant may request its bank to issue a letter of credit to the landlord as security. In such a transaction, the tenant is the applicant, the bank is the issuer and the landlord is the beneficiary.

Leverage - Leverage is the use of various financial instruments or borrowed capital to increase the potential return of an investment – and it is an extremely common term on both Wall Street and in the Main Street real estate market. (Learn more about the various uses of leverage in Leveraged Investment Showdown.)

Like kind property - Like-Kind Property. Any two assets or properties that are considered to be the same type, making an exchange between them tax free. To qualify as like kind, two assets must be of the same type (e.g. two pieces of residential real estate), but do not have to be of the same quality.

Limited partnership - RELP' A limited partnership entity organized to invest in real estate. A Real Estate Limited Partnership is typically organized with an experienced property manager or real estate development firm serving as the general partner.

Lis pendens - In United States law, a lis pendens is a written notice that a lawsuit has been filed concerning real estate, involving either the title to the property or a claimed ownership interest in it.

Loan to value - The loan to value or LTV ratio of a property is the percentage of the property's value that is mortgaged. ... Loan to Value is used in commercial real estate as well. Examples: $300,000 appraised value of a home. $240,000 mortgage on the property. $240,000 / $300,000 = .80 or 80% Loan to Value Ratio

Market value - Market value is the most probable price that a property should bring in a competitive and open market under all conditions requisite to a fair sale, the buyer and seller, each acting prudently, knowledgeably and assuming the price is not affected by undue stimulus.

Mechanics lien - A guarantee of payment to builders, contractors and construction firms that build or repair structures. Mechanic's liens also extend to suppliers of materials and subcontractors and cover building repairs as well.

Mortgage broker - A mortgage broker is an intermediary working with a borrower and a lender while qualifying the borrower for a mortgage. The broker gathers income, asset and employment documentation, a credit report and other information for assessing the borrower's ability to secure financing.

Multiple listing - A multiple listing service (MLS, also multiple listing system or multiple listings service) is a suite of services that real estate brokers use to establish contractual offers of compensation (among brokers) and accumulate and disseminate information to enable appraisals.

Net income - Net operating income (NOI) is a calculation used to analyze real estate investments that generate income. Net operating income equals all revenue from the property minus all reasonably necessary operating expenses

Net rentable area - Actual square-unit of a building that may be leased or rented to tenants, the area upon which the lease or rental payments are computed. It usually excludes common areas, elevator shafts, stairways, and space devoted to cooling, heating, or other equipment. Also called net leasable area.

Non-recourse note - Nonrecourse debt or a nonrecourse loan is a secured loan (debt) that is secured by a pledge of collateral, typically real property, but for which the borrower is not personally liable.

Obsolescence - Functional obsolescence is a reduction in the usefulness or desirability of an object because of an outdated design feature, usually one that cannot be easily changed. The term is commonly used in real estate, but has a wide application.

Option - A real estate purchase option is a contract on a specific piece of real estate that allows the buyer the exclusive right to purchase the property. Once a buyer has an option to buy a property, the seller cannot sell the property to anyone else.

Passive activity income - Internal Revenue Service (IRS) defines two types of passive activity: trade or business activities not materially participated in, and rental activities even if the taxpayer materially participated in them (unless the taxpayer is a real estate professional).

Point - In real estate mortgages, a point refers to the origination fee charged by the lender, with each point being equal to 1% of the amount of the loan. It can also refer to each percentage difference between a mortgage's interest rate and the prime interest rate.

Possession - A principle of real estate law that allows a person who possesses someone else's land for an extended period of time to claim legal title to that land.

Potential gross income - The amount of income produced by a piece of property, plus miscellaneous income, less vacancy costs and collection losses. Effective gross income is a metric commonly used to evaluate the value of a piece of investment property. ... The EGI for the property is $500,000 - $100,000, or $400,000.

Preliminary title report - A preliminary title sets forth various details about a piece of real estate, including: Ownership;

Liens and encumbrances; and Easements.

The information in a preliminary title report, also known as a title search, is gathered from the property records in the county where the property is located.

Prepayment penalty - Prepayment Penalty. A prepayment penalty is a clause in a mortgage contract stating that a penalty will be assessed if the mortgage is prepaid within a certain time period. The penalty is based on a percentage of the remaining mortgage balance or a certain number of months' worth of interest.

Principal - In commercial law, a principal is a person, legal or natural, who authorizes an agent to act to create one or more legal relationships with a third party.

Pro forma - What does 'Pro Forma' mean. Pro forma, a Latin term, literally means "for the sake of form" or "as a matter of form." In the world of investing, pro forma refers to a method by which financial results are calculated. This method of calculation places emphasis on present or projected figures.

Promissory note - In the United States, a mortgage note (also known as a real estate lien note, borrower's note) is a promissory note secured by a specified mortgage loan; it is a written promise to repay a specified sum of money plus interest at a specified rate and length of time to fulfill the promise.

Property management - Property management is the operation, control, and oversight of real estate as used in its most broad terms. Management indicates a need to be cared for, monitored and accountability given for its useful life and condition.

Quit claim deed - A quitclaim deed is a legal instrument which is used to transfer interest in real property. The entity transferring its interest is called the grantor, and when the quitclaim deed is properly completed and executed, it transfers any interest the grantor has in the property to a recipient, called the grantee.

Real estate owned (REO) - Real estate owned or REO is a term used in the United States to describe a class of property owned by a lender—typically a bank, government agency, or government loan insurer—after an unsuccessful sale at a foreclosure auction.

Real property - Real estate is "property consisting of land and the buildings on it, along with its natural resources such as crops, minerals or water; immovable property of this nature; an interest vested in this (also) an item of real property, (more generally) buildings or housing in general.

Realized gain - The amount by which the sale price of an asset exceeds its purchase price. Unless the realized gain came from a tax-exempt or tax-deferred asset, it is taxable. However, the type of taxation to which it is subject varies according to how long the asset has been owned. A realized gain from an asset owned longer than one year is usually taxed at the capital gains rate, while an asset owned for a period shorter than a year is often subject to the higher income tax rate. It is also called the recognized gain.

Refinancing - Getting a new mortgage to replace the original is called refinancing. Refinancing is done to allow a borrower to obtain a better interest term and rate. The first loan is paid off, allowing the second loan to be created, instead of simply making a new mortgage and throwing out the original mortgage.

Rental concession - Rental Concessions are benefits that are offered by the landlord to his tenants. Concessions are usually offered to draw tenants to vacant properties. Some other landlords may choose to offer a concession if the tenant decides to renew the lease. Even when the landlord is planning to sell a home, in return for his tenants co-operation he may offer incentives or concessions.

Replacement cost - A replacement cost is the cost to replace an asset of a company at the same or equal value, and the asset to be replaced could be a building, investment securities, accounts receivable or liens.

Reproduction cost - The costs involved with identically reproducing an asset or property with the same materials and specifications as an insured property based on current prices.

Rescission - Rescission is the cancellation of a real estate contract between the buyer and seller. The act of rescinding a contract will "unwind" the transaction specified in the contract. A real estate contract may be rescinded at varying points during a transaction.

Restrictive covenant - A restrictive covenant is any type of agreement that requires the buyer to either take or abstain from a specific action. In real estate transactions, restrictive covenants are binding legal obligations written into the deed of a property by the seller.

Right of survivorship - The right of survivorship is an attribute of several types of joint ownership of property, most notably joint tenancy and tenancy in common. When jointly owned property includes a right of survivorship, the surviving owner automatically absorbs a dying owner's share of the property. Thus if A and B jointly own a house with a right of survivorship, and B dies, A becomes the sole owner of the house, despite any contrary intent in B's will.

Secondary mortgage market - A secondary mortgage market is the market where mortgage loans and servicing rights are bought and sold between mortgage originators, mortgage aggregators (securitizers) and investors. The secondary mortgage market is extremely large and liquid.

Short-rate - The relatively higher insurance premium rate charged for coverage when one cancels a policy earlier than originally agreed upon. Rather than receiving a pro rata refund of the unearned premium,the property owner receives a smaller amount.

Standby commitment - A standby commitment is a formal agreement by a bank agreeing to lend money to a borrower up to a specified amount for a specific period. It is also known as firm commitment lending. The amount given under standby commitment is to be used only in specified contingency.

Subject to mortgage - circumstance in which a buyer takes title to mortgaged real property but is not personally liable for the payment of the amount due. The buyer must make payments in order to keep the property; however, with default, only the buyer's equity in that property is lost. Contrast assumption of mortgage.

Subordination - For an individual, the most frequent example of a subordination agreement is when an individual attempts to refinance the first mortgage on a property which has a second mortgage. The second mortgage has a lower priority than the first mortgage, but these priorities may be upset by refinancing the loan.

Supply and demand - The law of supply and demand is a basic economic principle that explains the relationship between supply and demand for a good or service and how the interaction affects the price of that good or service. The relationship of supply and demand affects the housing market and the price of a house

Tax lien - A tax lien is a lien imposed by law upon a property to secure the payment of taxes. A tax lien may be imposed for delinquent taxes owed on real property or personal property, or as a result of failure to pay income taxes or other taxes.

Tax shelter -Tax shelters can range from investments or investment accounts that provide favorable tax ... evasion, the illegal avoidance of taxes through misrepresentation or similar means. ... A tax shelter product designed to create large, seemingly real .

Tenancy by entirety - Tenants by entirety (TBE) is a method in some states by which married couples can hold the title to a property. In order for one spouse to modify his or her interest in the property in any way, the consent of both spouses is required by tenants by entirety.

Tenants-in-common - Tenancy in common is a type of shared ownership of property, where each owner owns a share of the property. Unlike in a joint tenancy, these shares can be of unequal size, and can be freely transferred to other owners both during life and via a will.

Title - a right or claim to the ownership of property or to a rank or throne.

Title insurance policy - Title insurance is an insurance policy that covers the loss of ownership interest in a property due to legal defects and is required if the property is under mortgage. The most common type of title insurance is a lender's title insurance, which is paid for by the borrower but protects only the lender.

Trust deed - a deed of conveyance creating and setting out the conditions of a trust

Usury - the illegal action or practice of lending money at unreasonably high rates of interest.

Vacancy and rent loss - Vacancy and Credit Loss in real estate investing is the amount of money or percentage of net operating income that is estimated to not be realized due to non-payment of rents and vacant units

Vacancy factor - The vacancy rate is the percentage of all available units in a rental property, such as a hotel or apartment complex, that are vacant or unoccupied at a particular time. It is the opposite of the occupancy rate, which is the percentage of units in a rental property that are occupied.

Warranty deed - a deed that guarantees a clear title to the buyer of real property.

Will - A will or testament is a legal document by which a person, the testator, expresses their wishes as to how their property is to be distributed at death, and names one or more persons, the executor, to manage the estate until its final distribution.

Without recourse - a formula used to disclaim responsibility for future nonpayment, especially of a negotiable financial instrument.

Wrap-around - "wrap", is a form of secondary financing for the purchase of real property. The seller extends to the buyer a junior mortgage which wraps around and exists in addition to any superior mortgages already secured by the property.

Please Leave a Great Review!

I have purchased all of the top real estate investing books on the market, and most have a handful of out dated web sites for their sources of properties.

There is not another real estate investing book on the market that gives you as many sources for wholesale real estate than this book.

My book gives you more and in most cases for less!

I have enjoyed doing all the research and sharing my real world real estate investing experience in what I hope is easy to understand terminology.

So I ask you to leave a honest and hopefully great review!

Thank you. Warm Regards,

Brian Mahoney

Amazon Review

Get Our Massive Money Complete Internet Marketing Video Training Program at:

(Zero Cost Internet Marketing complete 142 video series)

$1,997 Megasized Money Making Marketing Program

ONLY $67 !!!!

https://goo.gl/Qed1dY

Made in the USA
San Bernardino, CA
29 February 2020

65158191R00069